IMAGES
of Scotland

THE CLYDE SUBMARINE BASE

HMS *King George* V, aground on Rhu Narrows. This picture probably explains the why the Admiralty insisted that Faslane should be a base for submarines when it opened.

IMAGES
of Scotland

THE CLYDE SUBMARINE BASE

Compiled by
Keith Hall

All the royalties from the sale of this book will be
donated to the Royal Naval Submarine Museum
(Registered Charity No.1068419)

TEMPUS

First published 1999
Copyright © Keith Hall, 1999

Tempus Publishing Limited
The Mill, Brimscombe Port,
Stroud, Gloucestershire, GL5 2QG

ISBN 0 7524 1657 X

Typesetting and origination by
Tempus Publishing Limited
Printed in Great Britain by
Midway Clark Printing, Wiltshire

HMS *Vanguard* passing through Rhu Narrows on her way to Faslane. On 12 August 1960 she was taken over by Metal Industries to be scrapped.

Contents

Acknowledgements

I would like to thank the following for their help and assistance in compiling this book: FOSNI Photographic Section, for their patience, professionalism and allowing me to rummage; Major D. Dow and Mr M. Reeves; Mr G. McFeely for his encouragement, friendly advice and allowing me to draw on the content of his own publication, HM Naval Base Clyde, 1996; Mr J. Drummond from the Facilities Department and the staff of EWC (SERCO) for allowing me 'free rein' in their photographic archives; the staff of Paper Clip, Helensburgh for their patience and expertise in reproducing the majority of the pictures that make up this book, Rolls-Royce and associates for their help in gathering information on the early days of the nuclear programme, and Mr Ronnie Dick for his skill in developing the pictures that seemed beyond redemption. My thanks also to Commander Tall and his staff at the Royal Naval Submarine Museum, Gosport.

I am particularly grateful to the following organizations for permission to use their photographs and the waiving of their copyright fee:

Crown Copyright, for all the MOD photographs;

The Royal Commission on the Ancient and Historical Monuments of Scotland (MOD Collection), for the photographs on pages 34/35 and 110(top);

The Imperial War Museum, for the photographs on pages 20, 22, 23(top), 32, 33 and 36;

John Gurthrie Aerial Photography, for the photographs on pages 100 to 106;

Scottish Media Newspapers, for the photograph on page 110(bottom);

Clyde & Forth Press Ltd, for the items on pages 49 and 56;

Mr R. Preston, for the photograph on page 11(top);

Mr C. Anderson, for the photographs on pages 2 and 4;

Mr Allan Carvanna for permission to use his father's photographs (Mr William Carvanna), who was a foreman at Metal Industries. The photographs are on pages 39 to 41 and 42(top).

I am also greatly indebted to Commodore R.J. Lord MSc, Royal Navy (Director Naval Base Clyde) for his permission to tell this story and Tempus Publishing for the opportunity to share it with you.

And finally, to a submariners wife, Hilary, for being this submariner's wife.

Foreword

I am delighted to endorse this account of the Clyde Submarine Base and its history. Having been involved in the base during the very early Polaris days and recently returning as the Director, it is very clear to me that the publishing of this book goes some way towards filling a void in the noble story of a vibrant industrial and support establishment. I have found the book a fascinating reading and have drawn from it in the many presentations on the base that I give.

I consider that this record is especially important in these times of rapid change; it allows us not only to reflect on the past but also to focus on the present and the future of a facility in which all those involved can be justifiably proud.

Having the honour of serving as Director Naval Base Clyde, I commend this publication to you, knowing that it will jog both submariners' and base personnel's memories and allow them to retrace steps and remember friends who otherwise might be forgotten.

Commodore R.J. Lord MSc, Royal Navy

Introduction

It is a product of imaginative brains, not only in the blueprint, but as a result of meticulous planning. Nothing can detract from its marvellous achievement. It will ever be a monument to our unconquerable spirit in face of great odds in defence in our way of living. It was a challenge.

So wrote Mr McPhail about the Military Port at Faslane, in Helensburgh and the three Lochs.

But why write about a submarine base and why this one in particular? Firstly, I have spent the majority of my working life at Faslane. I met the lady who was to become my wife when I returned from an operational submarine patrol to Faslane. I sailed from Faslane when I went to fight my war, and fortuitously returned safely when it was all over. My children also grew up on the lochside. Secondly, I would like to take this opportunity to remember all those friends and old comrades who over the years put so much into this book, but couldn't wait around to see it published.

This small book, however, is not intended as a historical narrative. The earlier works of Maughan and McPhail tell of the area's past in greater depth and detail and, if the truth were told, probably in better English. Their style of writing is enchanting, but such elegant prose does not come easily to a 'macho submariner', or the author for that matter.

The base has witnessed many changes over the years. Three times it has been the largest building site in the United Kingdom, if not Europe. Hopefully this book will record, in part, the changes to the base since it was first constructed over fifty years ago, and archive and put on record some of the photographs associated with the base's proud past. Apart from enjoying the book and stirring memories, I hope it might encourage some readers to delve into their own collections of photographs and share them, for these old pictures are now 'the keepers of the past'.* It is difficult to predict what the future may bring for either the base in particular, or the Royal Navy in general. However, one thing we can be sure of is that without a past there is no future and we cannot remember the future.

The term 'the Navy I joined' is an expression I often hear. Whether or not this mythical place exists anywhere other than in our imagination is open to debate, but wherever your Navy may be, I hope this book will, in some small way, help you find it or at least remember it.

Keith Hall
Tumbledown

* The submarine museum at Gosport would make a fine and fitting resting place for them.

One

Before 1939

During the 1500s, it is said, 'a saurian monster arrived in the loch, with a long straight giraffe-like neck, having a tail like that of a crocodile that could break an oak tree'. Tradition recounts that it travelled at great speed. 'It did everything horrible except spit fire from its ugly jaws. Everyone was panic stricken and knelt on the shores praying to be delivered from this evil leviathan of the depths of the oceans'. Even to this day there are among us those who understand, and would agree with the sentiments of the last sentence.

Since those dark days, things have improved somewhat on the lochside. During the mid-1800s the Gareloch and surrounding district had become a much-favoured residential area by Glasgow-based professional and business people. Many imposing mansions were built along the Gareloch during the prosperous years in the middle of the nineteenth century, and piers were built to encourage potential house builders to move into the area. At this time, the Gareloch had no fewer than eight piers. A little later, the West Highland Railway opened, initially hoping to win passengers away from the steamers or private coaches. At the time, there were four trains daily between the lochside stations and Craigendoran. Unfortunately, the approaches to the railway stations were long and steep, due to them being sited above the villages on the hillside. One disgruntled passenger wrote in the Railway Herald: 'Sound heart and lungs and experience in hill climbing are essential to a man who hurries from the breakfast table to catch a train at one of the lochside stations. It is easier to go to the pier'.

At Shandon, seventeen large houses were built. The most impressive, West Shandon House, was built for Robert Napier, the eminent shipbuilder and engineer. From 1833, he had a summer cottage at Shandon and by 1846 he took up a permanent residence building for himself and his family, a majestic home on the site of the smaller cottage. By 1852 the house accommodated Napier's extensive collection of valuable antiques and paintings. David Livingston, the explorer and a close friend of Napier's, would bring him flora and plants collected on his travels. As a result, the grounds and gardens were very impressive. After Napier's death in 1876, the house and its contents were sold for £38,000. It was bought by a company who enlarged it and ran it as a successful Hydropathic Establishment. It was advertised as providing 'Russian, Turkish and saltwater swimming baths, covered and open tennis courts. Additionally, a golf course, croquet and bowling green were available to patrons, all this for eighteen shillings a day!' It stood roughly where the new Warrent Officers and Senior Rates Mess now stands.

During the First World War the Navy took possession of the 'Hydro' for use as a hospital. After the war it returned to being a hotel. During the Second World War, the hotel was handed over to the Army and the grounds cleared to make way for army huts. Similar camps were built at Stuckenduff, Blairvadoch, Faslane and Bendarroch. After this war the 'Hydro' once again returned to its former occupation, but this proved unsuccessful. The house fell into disrepair and was eventually demolished in 1958. Apart from the monumental retaining wall and its turrets which can still be seen alongside the southern approach road to the base, very little remains of this imposing house. In the woods behind the MOD houses on the eastern side of the A814, which were part of the Hydro's gardens, can still be seen the ponds that supplied the house with water and the foundations of a gazebo. The Southern Gatehouse stands on the southern approach road, which was, at the time, the main trunk road to the west.

To the northern end of the base stands another imposing residence, Belmore House, currently employed as the First Submarine Squadron's headquarters. Belmore was built in the early 1830s by a local fisherman, Mr McFarlane. The house was originally a small two-storey house, and was sold some years later to Mr Honeyman, who added considerably to the basic structure. The house was acquired in 1856 by Mr McDonald, who remodelled the mansion to give it the appearance it now has. Belmore at this time was famed for its gardens.

Further to the north in Faslane Cemetery are the ancient remains of a chapel dedicated to St. Michael. It was here that Robert the Bruce is said to have sought peaceful retirement. To the east of the cemetery is where Faslane Castle once stood. Tradition dictates that William Wallace rested there after 'destroying the Castle of Rosneath'. This small cemetery also contains a memorial to the contractors and members of the crew of the submarine K13, who perished in an accident at Faslane Bay on 29 January 1917. The submarine had left the builders yard that morning to carry out acceptance trials. Intended as the first Fleet submarines, the K class were large steam turbine-powered submarines. At 320ft long and displacing 3,200 tons, their 1,000hp engines gave them a speed of 24 knots on the surface. The turbine engines were powered by two oil-fired boilers, which required large ventilators in the form of two funnels, lowered and sealed before the submarine dived. During the trials she sank in 64ft of water taking eighty-three members of the combined service and civilian crew with her. Desperate efforts were made to salvage the submarine and some fifty-six hours later the bow was raised clear of the water and a hole was cut enabling the personnel in the for'd section to escape. Fortunately, forty-eight men were saved this way. Six weeks later the boat was raised and recommissioned as K23; she was finally scrapped in 1926. A memorial service is still held at Rhu church every year to mark the tragic anniversary of the accident and at Faslane Cemetery by Service personnel from HMS *Neptune*.

The Gareloch was used as a 'ship park' on several occasions. This picture was taken in the early 1930s and shows the original shoreline at Faslane Bay.

Ardencaple Castle, the ancestral home of the clan MacAulay.

Ardencaple Castle. The remains of the West Tower can still be seen in the Naval married quarters, as can the massive retaining wall that fronted the castle.

The shore road at Rhu.

Above and below (background): The *Empress*, an ex Royal Naval warship (HMS *Revenge*), in the Gareloch off Rhu. The ship was effectively a floating reform school that could cater for up to 400 boys. It was paid for by several leading Glasgow businessmen and replaced the *Cumberland* which they had moved to the loch for this purpose in 1897. This first shiphad lasted until 1889 when, allegedly, she was set alight by some of the boys.

LMORE ROAD. FASLANE, GARELOCH.

The lochside road, by Belmore House.

The shore road, near Garelochhead.

A group of J class yachts racing on the loch.

West Shandon, as it was built by Robert Napier, engineer and shipbuilder.

The Shandon Hydro, as seen from the loch.

The Hydro terrace overlooking the Gareloch

The Hydro's South Lodge was a post office for a number of years. It latterly became a general store to cater for the growing service population, and families were housed in a caravan park in the grounds of the Hydro.

An interior view of the Hydro, showing the second lounge.

Two
1939-1945

At the outbreak of the Second World War, it was expected that Britain would suffer almost immediate bombing raids by the German airforce. The first bombs to fall on mainland Britain were at Canterbury on 9 May 1940. The Orkneys had come under attack as early as 17 October 1939. After the fall of France, in June 1940, the battle for air supremacy over the Channel and Southern England started in earnest. By October 1940, the Luftwaffe conceded RAF supremacy and changed their tactics accordingly. Enemy night air raids started with all major British ports as their principle targets.

This scenario had been anticipated. In 1936 a subcommittee of the Committee of Imperial Defence had formed Emergency Committees in all the principal ports. Their main aim was to maximize capacity in the remaining harbours, should one or more of the ports become inoperable due to enemy bombing. On 7 July 1940, Major General Riddel-Webster wrote a memo summarizing the Army's position. It emphasized the need to increase military capacity in existing ports and create new berths. A meeting was held at the War Office on 12 July 1940 where it was decided to explore both these options. A group was formed with representatives from the Military, Ministry of Shipping and the LMS. In the course of their research they visited Barrow, Maryport, Ardrossan, Craigendoran, Gareloch and Oban. The committee decided that only three options were worth further investigation:

a. Oban, although at the three local sites selected at Oban, the quay length was limited.

b. The eastern shore of Loch Ryan at Cairnryan, which would allow the necessary berths to be built and was near the deep water channel. The railway system serving the area was limited, however, and a bulk of the traffic would have to pass through Carlisle.

c. The Gareloch, a deep water, sheltered enclosure with ample manoeuvring room. Two possible sites were considered at the northern end of the loch, Mambeg and Faslane Bay. Mambeg, on the western side of the loch, would be a difficult site to pile because of rock close to the shore. Rail access would be difficult and because of lack of room at Mambeg the marshalling yard would still need to be on the opposite shore at Faslane.

The committee recommended, therefore that the Military Port be built at Faslane. The inability to pile at Mambeg and the time it would take to construct the railway track round the loch head contributed to making Faslane Bay the preferred option.

A meeting was called on the 27 August to discuss the findings of the report. Most of the Ministries were present at this meeting, although the Ministry of Labour did not attend and for sometime after, raised several objections to the proposed port. Ernest Bevin (the Minister) did not like the idea of a port run by the Military. It was thus decided to start construction at both sites, Faslane and Loch Ryan. Faslane was the preferred site; it would require the shortest line to connect it to the existing railway system, it was within the Clyde air defence area, and it was

In 1941 materials for the new port were starting to arrive.

assumed that partial use could be made of the port while construction continued. It was estimated that the total cost of construction at the Faslane site would be between £1.25 million and £1.75 million.

During February 1941, some 1,000 men were engaged in the building at Faslane, while at the same time at Loch Ryan they were only forty. During the spring of 1941, both Liverpool and Clydeside were heavily bombed. Authorization was given to build three extra deep water berths, both at Faslane and Cairnryan, bringing both ports up to the six berths originally intended. The construction work at Faslane was progressing well, despite the lack of barges and tugs, and problems with dredging the 'narrows' at Rhu.

Despite optimistic claims by the Ministry of War Transport, the port was not in a position to appoint a Superintendent (Colonel Bailey) until 6 April 1942, and it was not until midsummer that it could deal with large cargo vessels. The port was officially opened by the Secretary of State for the Ministry of War Transport on 8 August 1942.

Faslane by any standards was a significant port. Its six berths were all capable of handling vessels of 33ft maximum draught. It was provided with capacious lighterage quays and had an impressive array of cranage, some thirty-six shore cranes and a 150 ton floating crane. A 35,000 ton battleship could be berthed and over 1,500 railway goods wagons could be accommodated in the sidings at Faslane Bay.

The Clyde Navigation Trust (CNT), which represented the interests of the existing Clyde Ports, expressed concern over the Military Port on two accounts; firstly the Clyde ports had already invested large sums of money in extending their facilities to cope with the increase in war traffic, and secondly, the military port posed a very real threat, once the war was over, as a rival. To alleviate these fears, the Regional Port Director wrote in January 1942 that:

a.   The port would only be operated by Service personnel.

b.   It would not be used for handling commercial cargos as long as commercial berths were available.

c.   When the war was over the port would not be sold or leased without consultation with the CNT.

This assurance was to cause problems on several occasions during the port's wartime career. For example; a deck cargo of aircraft and 2,339 mailbags of US government mail were delayed when the military refused to unload them, and special indemnities had to be raised before this particular cargo could be dealt with.

As the war progressed, it became apparent that the Atlantic coast ports were not being subjected to the extent of enemy bombing that had been envisaged at the outbreak of the war. As a result Faslane had redundant capacity. With the preparations for Operation Overlord (the invasion of Europe) on the south coast and the vast amount of stores required, the War Office felt the skilled dock troops could be better deployed. In March 1943, Faslane (Military Port No.1), was manned by twenty-five HQ staff, 200 men on port maintenance, 150 in the Wharfmasters' section, 180 on cargo securing and 200 operating the port railway. The Government asked the railway companies to take over the running of the port railways, but the companies declined and left the War Department (WD) with little option other than to scale down its operations at the military ports. From February 1944, Cairnryan was put on a care and maintenance basis, and the number of staff at Faslane greatly decreased. The requirement at Faslane was to retain the lighterage wharf, two deep water berths and the 150 ton crane; it would also be needed for the troopship movements connected with Operation Overlord. The War Department railway handled its first passenger train on the 5 August 1943 when Winston Churchill embarked from the port for the USA. In March 1945, the War Office stated that Military Port No.1 (Faslane) would not be needed after the war had ended in Europe. Military Port No.2 (Cairnryan) could cope with the Army's needs for training and with the war against Japan. Considerable pressure was put on the Government to ensure that the promises made during the conflict, about Faslane not being sold as a commercial port, were kept. In April 1945, the War Office decided that the site should be leased to a ship-breaking firm. Although this decision pleased the CNT, it did not suit everyone. A firm of freight brokers, who had an office at Faslane, wanted to continue its operations, and the railway companies suggested Faslane would be a suitable location to undertake the now long overdue wagon repairs, using Prisoner of War (POW) labour. The discussions dragged on and the Army, against this background of uncertainty, announced the port would close for all operations on 31 March 1946.

The marshalling yard at what is now the northern end of the base.

Faslane Bay, 1941. The piling for the lighterage jetty is almost complete, and the infilling is well under way. For the train spotters: it is an ex-GWR Deans in the back ground.

Looking south down the Gareloch.

The port from the loch.

The deep water berths.

Looking north along the deep water berths. The floating crane is alongside a ship.

Railway wagons on the jetties.

A ship being unloaded at the deep water berths.

Military Port No.1, as seen from the loch. Belmore House can be seen on the left.

Aircraft being unloaded at the deep water berths.

Looking over the railway line towards the deep water quays.

Looking towards Garelochhead, the marshalling yard can be seen behind the quay.

The port looking across Faslane Bay.

The deep water berths.

Balernock House stood where the wardroom tennis courts are now

Above and below: Two views of Belmore House.

Belmore House is now the offices of the First Submarine Squadron.

The Army 'messing about' in boats.

The Military Port from the loch. Perhaps as a divine forecast of the better days to come, these cranes were used to unload the first X craft (X3) from a specially constructed railway truck.

The Spud pontoon approaching the floating pier! 'Must be an Army thing.'

Following pages: This photograph was taken in 1947 and shows the military activity around what is now the south end of the base.

General Sir Bernard C.T. Paget KCB, DSO, MC, Commander-in-Chief, Home Forces, accompanied by Colonel C.A. Bailey (Port Superintendent), inspects the port during December 1942.

Three
1945-1960

Tenders to lease the Faslane site were received from three ship breaking firms: Metal Industries were clearly the favoured choice and, during April 1946, discussions began in earnest with the Company.

The firm sent the Government an offer to lease the site and purchase the plant on 22 July 1946, for £102,500. The offer was accepted and the Company took over the lease from 31 July. The former Military Port was formally handed over to the Ministry of Transport Port and Canal Directorate on 15 August 1946 and from Ministry to Metal Industries on the same day. This handover procedure was later to cause many problems when the Government assessed an undervaluation of the site by some £100,000.

Most of the Royal Navy's capital ships were laid up in the Gareloch in the mid-1950s. On 15 July 1956 some 200,000 tons of Naval vessels were awaiting disposal in the loch. These included three battleships, two aircraft carriers and the cruiser *Swiftsure*. The majority of the workers at the Metal Industries Faslane site were Polish, displaced after the Second World War, and who lived on site in the former Army huts.

The Germans were conducting experiments with closed cycle propulsion systems that were independent of the outside atmosphere as early as 1911. In 1940, following the successful trials of the hydrogen peroxide (HPT) powered V 80, a number of similarly powered submarines were built. During 1946 one of these submarines, U 1407, which had been scuttled at Cuxhaven after the German collapse, was salvaged and commissioned into the Royal Navy as HMS *Meteorite*. Originally built by Blohm and Voss and launched in 1943, she was raised in May 1946 at Cuxhaven for evaluation of the Walther HPT turbine. Professor Walther and his staff came from Germany to Barrow to advise Vickers engineers during the rebuilding. Vickers were given the task of carrying out the evaluation, and on the strength of their report the two Ex class submarines were ordered.

The principle of the HPT system was a closed circuit turbine powered by gas, independent of the external atmosphere. The gas was generated by the decomposition in water of concentrated hydrogen peroxide (Perhydral or Ingolin). Fuel consumption was high and the compound unstable. HMS *Meteorite* was finally broken up at Barrow in September 1949 by T.W. Ward Ltd.

In 1954 a shore support building for the HPT boats was built at Faslane. The building still exists today and until recently was supplying power to submarines as the Southern Utilities Building (SUB).

The trials with HMS *Meteorite* led to a development programme in which two HPT-powered, 1,120 ton submarines were built by Vickers at Barrow in Furnace. They were purely experimental submarines, unarmed but impressively fast, with submerge speeds in excess of 25 knots. Experiencing many teething troubles, HMS *Explorer's* first Captain never took her to sea. The HPT was an unpredictable fuel at best. There were several reports of explosions onboard the submarines and on more than one occasion the crew had to 'abandon' ship and stand on the casing to escape the choking fumes that filled the submarine's interior. The High

Test Peroxide was a very volatile substance, stowed external to the hull in special bags, which sometimes exploded while the submarine was underway. While the submarines were at sea, the engine room was normally unmanned, which was probably a sensible state, as it was not unusual to see fire balls 'dancing' along the tops of the combustion chambers. One member of the crew of an HPT boat remarked, 'I think the best thing we can do with peroxide is to try to get it adopted by potential enemies'.

As the nuclear programme got underway, the HPT boats became redundant and were scrapped in 1969-1970, eventually being broken-up in Barrow. The periscope from HMS *Explorer* ended up in the Periscope Pub on Walney Island. It was taken out a few years ago after a number of complaints from locals who thought pub-goers were using the periscope to look into their bedrooms and bathrooms!

Ex-class
Displacement surfaced: 780 tons
Displacement dived: 1,000 tons
Dimensions; 225½ x 15½ x 11
Complement: *Explorer*-49, *Excalibur*-41
Propulsion: diesel engines, electric motors and steam turbines
Speed surfaced: 15 knots
Speed dived: 30 knots.

On 9 Sept 1957 HMS *Adamant* and her flotilla of submarines left Rothesay to take part in a NATO exercise. On 12 Oct 1957, HMS *Adamant* returned from the exercise and entered the Gareloch, accompanied by her squadron of submarines, two frigates and a floating dock, to establish the first British permanent submarine base in the loch. As the squadron grew, HMS *Ben Nevis* (a converted tank landing ship) joined the squadron to increase the availability of much needed accommodation. As a depot ship, HMS *Adamant* travelled with her submarines, a luxury not afforded to HMS *Neptune* when she took over the role as 'depot ship' some years later. On 27 Jun 1958, HMS *Adamant* returned to Faslane after visit to Bergen. HMS *Taciturn* and HMS *Truncheon* had accompanied her on the visit.

On 10 May 1958, HMS *Explorer* and HMS *Excalibur* joined the 3rd Submarine Squadron, Faslane. During July of this year, the old floating dock AFD 58 was sold to a Norwegian firm and removed from the loch. At this time the officers' mess was a thatched villa 'across the road' from the depot ship.

Faslane Port.

Part of the breaking yard.

The railway line approaching the breaking yard.

A busy scene at the yard.

HMS *Vanguard* at the breakers yard.

Ships anchored in the Gareloch prior to disposal. The four-funneled ship alongside at Faslane is the *Aquitania*.

HMS *Anson* in the loch. Garelochhead can be seen in the background.

THE GARELOCH FROM CLYNDER   D 2734

The loch viewed from Clynder.

The German First World War battleship *Derfflinger* being towed to the breakers yard – the ship is upside down in the floating dock.

The loch viewed from Garelochhead. Sadly, many ships can be seen waiting their turn to be scrapped.

The foundations of the Hydrogen Peroxide test shop, under construction in 1954.

The Hydrogen Peroxide production facility, nearing completion.

Ground preparation for the HPT building.

The HPT building almost complete. This building continues to operate as the Southern Utilities Building.

HMS *Metorite*.

The Submarine Base in the late 1950s.

HMS *Maidstone* alongside at Faslane.

The building at the right of the picture is the canteen.

1st Sailor: "Wish we'd never left Bute!"
2nd Sailor: "Me either, mate, I never got over me sea-sickness coming up."

THE GARELOCH FROM SHANDON CARAVAN PARK D 5441

Shandon caravan park, which was used as married quarters. One of the Submarine Squadron's frigates can be seen in the background.

HMS *Maidstone*, on a visit to Rotterdam

Divisions on HMS *Maidstone*.

HMS *Solent* passing through Rhu Narrows.

An Ex-class submarine, alongside their special refuelling jetty.

Four

1960-1980

As we set the scene for this era we should note that in February 1942 the German scientist Heisenberg gave a talk entitled 'The theory of extracting energy from uranium fission' at the Reich research council convention. At this seminar, he postulated that, because of the engine's independence of an external air supply, the most obvious use of this form of power would be to power a submarine.

After the Second World War the British Navy's efforts in submarine propulsion development were centred around the hydrogen peroxide steam turbine plant acquired from the Germans at the end of the war and further developed in the Ex-class submarines.

In 1946 Lord Portall was appointed Controller of Atomic Energy and Christopher Hinton set up the Production Group at Risley. An intensive atomic power research programme commenced at Harwell. By 1947 the first graphite-moderated reactor,'Gleep', went critical. Construction of the site at Sellafield was in service and by the end of 1950 the Windscale reactor was critical. In 1946 the Admiralty appointed Naval Officers and a member of the Royal Naval Scientific Service to the Atomic Energy Research Establishment at Harwell. The aim was to consider whether this form of power had any practical use for powering Royal Navy ships.

In 1955 the world's first nuclear powered submarine (USS *Nautilis*) was deployed. The Naval section at Harwell under Captain Harrison-Smith was placed on a more formal footing and work began in earnest. During the year, the staff was increased by personnel from the Royal Corps of Naval Constructors (RCNC) and engineers from Vickers Armstrong Ltd.

Because of the experimental nature of the work and following American practice, it was proposed to build a land-based prototype. In due course a site at Dounreay, Scotland, was chosen. The aim at this stage was to take the plant critical by January 1961. The Dounreay site was leased from the neighbouring United Kingdom Atomic Energy Authority (UKAEA) site, as they could also provide the necessary support services: electricity, radioactive waste disposal, medical services, etc. Primarily because of the limited space on board the submarines, the type of reactor chosen was the pressurised water reactor and the programme was intended to achieve submarine plant criticality by mid-1962. Construction of the Dounreay Submarine Prototype (DSMP1) and supporting facilities lasted from 1957 to 1965 and a Royal Naval presence was established from 1961. Initial start up of the prototype 'Valiant' plant took place in January 1965. The protracted programme was, in part, due to the discovery of cracks in the welds of small bore Inconel tubing, resulting in a major reappraisal of plant material and the introduction of stainless steel throughout the primary plant.

From the beginning of the programme, Rolls Royce Ltd were involved. At this stage, two other companies became involved: Vickers Armstrong (Engineers) Ltd, who were the main contractors for the prototype machinery, and Foster Wheeler Ltd, designers and manufactures of the reactor pressure vessel, steam generators and associated primary circuit. Rolls Royce were the main subcontractor responsible for the design and production of the reactor and its associated equipment. The three firms formed two groups: Vickers Nuclear Engineering Ltd, and the Combined Derby Team. The programme was co-ordinated by the Naval Section at Harwell with the UKAEA providing experimental facilities and finance to meet the increasing cost of the production programme.

During late August 1956, Admiral Rickover USN visited the UK and toured various sites involved in the UK Naval atomic energy programme. On his second visit, in May 1957, a limited exchange of information began between the two Navies. It was during this visit that the foundations were laid for the US/UK Agreement. Shortly after this visit a British delegation embarked on a two-week tour of US Facilities. During the first of Admiral Rickovers visits, USN SeaWolf (liquid sodium cooled reactor) developed a leak. A complicated code had been developed in order that information could be passed to the Admiral without compromising security. Unfortunately, the Admiral forgot the code, and not being well known for his patience, finished up yelling down the phone 'Just tell me in plain English!' It was during Rickover's visit in 1956 that he met Lord Mountbatten. The two men seem to have got on rather well and the result was the 1958 US/UK Agreement. The USA Atomic Energy Act (1954) severely limited the information and equipment which could be supplied to other nations. Although Rickover's remark to Mountbatten, ' whether the British Admiralty wanted to satisfy its pride or whether it desired to get a nuclear submarine as quickly as possible', may have set the tone for the future co-operation between the two nations, it was the launch of the Russian Sputniks in October and November 1957 which impressed the world and worried NATO in particular, that finally set the wheels in motion. Harold Macmillan, Sir Edward Plowden (AEA) and Sir Richard Powell (MOD) visited Washington and at the ensuing discussions it was suggested that Britain could procure a complete nuclear submarine propulsion plant. In January 1958 the necessary legislation was introduced to the Senate. There was some opposition to this Amendment, but Admiral Rickover spoke in favour of the arrangement. It was then proposed that a British company would buy the plant from an American company and install it in a British-built submarine. This company was Roll Royce and Associates (a combination of Rolls Royce Ltd, Vickers Armstrong (Engineers) Ltd and Foster Wheeler Ltd). President Eisenhower signed the necessary legislation on 22 July 1958. The reason why

HMS *Dreadnought* passing through Rhu Narrows. The old American Base buildings can be seen in the background at Rosneath

HMS *Dreadnought*, alongside HMS *Maidstone*.

Rickover was so keen to help the British may be judged from a letter he wrote in late 1957, talking about his support for the exchange of technology. He wrote, 'I did this because of my feeling of urgency about the international situation, my admiration for the British, and particularly my great liking for Admiral Mountbatten.'

HMS *Dreadnought* was launched by Her Majesty the Queen on Trafalgar Day, 21 October 1960, the submarine being a direct hybrid result of the 1958 Agreement. The submarine's hull and front end were entirely British and from the reactor aft to the main shaft, American. HMS *Dreadnought* was a particularly successful submarine, although, apart from exercises, she spent the majority of her time taking VIPs to sea, a floating exhibition of the benefits of nuclear power. One of her most endearing characteristics that was proudly displayed was when she was at high speed on the surface, going 'on the step'. The submarine would effectively plane, being able to maintain speed while reducing reactor power. Under the terms of the 1958 Agreement, American assistance and support stopped in 1962.

There is no doubt that the British experiments would have led to a working reactor. HMS *Valiant* and HMS *Warspite* were the first all-British nuclear powered submarines, although the reactor had many features of the American S5W reactor (S for Submarine, 5 for the generation of the design, W for Westinghouse the designer) as fitted in HMS *Dreadnought*. The steam plant was entirely British and had been on trial in the Dounreay prototype for a number of years. Unlike the S5W, the British plant was optimized for noise reduction, and a considerable degree of success was achieved, although the submarines were not as easy to maintain or operate as HMS *Dreadnought*.

During 1955, the US National Security Committee decided to develop a submarine-launched ballistic missile system (SLBM). Between 1955 and 1960, the Polaris missile was developed and by 1960 the first USN Polaris submarines were on patrol. On 10 July 1960, the

WAR AND PEACE — the District's Double Life.

AT FASLANE

ROCKET FIRING SUBS?

ARMED WITH POLARIS MISSILE

WHITEHALL'S LATEST WARLIKE GIMMICK FOR THE GARELOCH—A POLARIS MISSILE BASE! WILL SUBMARINES—OWNED AND MANNED BY THE UNITED STATES—CARRYING ATOMIC WARHEAD MISSILES—START OPERATING FROM THE GARE LOCH? THAT'S THE QUESTION GARE-LOCHSIDERS ARE ASKING SINCE THE NEWS BROKE LAST WEEK IN LONDON.

A Foreign Office spokesman has disclosed that discussions are taking place with the United States authorities about the use of British ports by American rocket firing submarines . . . AND THE GARELOCH HAS BEEN SUGGESTED.

If this startling move—to have them based at Faslane comes off—then this 16-mile stretch of Scottish loch will become one of the most heavily concentrated fortifications in the British Isles.

They will move in alongside defence installations like the N.A.T.O. and minesweeper bases at Rosneath, the main rocket supply base for the Hebrides at Rhu Hangars, an oil terminal, and one of Britain's forward line submarine Squadrons at Faslane.

The nuclear-powered subs carry the United States' latest Polaris missile on their casing. With Uncle Sam at the trigger, they are capable of firing from underwater.

The missile can be discharged from about 90 ft. below the surface. Nuclear subs like the "George Washington" already carry up to 16 of these Polaris rocket missiles. They have a range of 1,500 miles and are fired in a two-stage rocket.

Launched from the Gareloch such a weapon could strike well into Russian-held territory.

The Foreign Office has pointed out that no agreement at present on "any particular project" has been reached.

It is particularly emphasised that the Americans do not wish to establish bases here, in the sense of taking over Royal Navy establishments, but negotiations are for the use of the ports for "replenishment" of such submarines.

At Faslane this week United States Naval Officer, Commander

AT SHANDON

FLOATING HOTEL

"Empress of France" Mentioned in Vast Schen

RUMOURS THAT THE 20,000-TON "EMPRESS OF FRA WILL BE MOORED IN THE GARELOCH AS A FLOA HOTEL HAVE BEEN HEARD IN GLASGOW SHIPPING CIR

The plan—to anchor a giant ocean-going liner close to the at Shandon and build an access ramp for tourists and ho makers—has been discussed.

A spokesman for Canadian Pacific Steamships Ltd wh the Empress at present on the Liverpool to Montreal run sai week . . .

"We have been approached about the scheme. But we don' it is feasible. If we sell the ship we will sell her to the l bidder."

The Empress of France was launched in the 1920's. She between 700 and 800 passengers.

The idea has been placed before the Scottish Tourist Bo includes the possibility of a helicopter service from Prestwick

Front page from the *Helensburgh Advertiser*, 5 August 1960. Shortly after this announcement about American ballistic missile submarines using the Faslane Base, Dunoon was informed on 1 November 1960 by Harold Macmillan that 'there would be an operational advantage, and that the deterrent would thereby be strengthened if a sheltered anchorage on this side of the Atlantic could be provided for a submarine depot ship and a floating dock, and that Her Majesty's Government have undertaken to provide this anchorage in the Holy Loch.'

first underwater launch of a Polaris missile from USS *George Washington* took place. Development work continued on the missile and by 1962 the A2 version was introduced. This in turn was replaced in 1964 by the A3. In its final stages of development, the Polaris A3 missile had a range of 2,500 miles and could deliver 3,200 kiloton warheads. The first test flight of the A3 took place at Cape Kennedy on 7 August 1962.

In 1952 Britain exploded its first nuclear weapon at Monte Bello. During this period a search for suitable delivery system for the weapon continued. Between 1952 and 1968, Britain's nuclear deterrent was the responsibility of the RAF, carried as either free-fall or air-launched intermediate range missiles. During the mid-1950s, Britain developed its own ballistic delivery system, known as the Blue Streak Project, but it was eventually cancelled. Work started on another system, Blue Water, but this again was cancelled in 1962. The cancellation of these programmes led to the decision to purchase an 'off the shelf' system from the US.

The first agreement between the US and Britain was for the purchase of the Sky Bolt ballistic missile under development in the US. However, in the early 1960s the Americans cancelled the Sky Bolt project. On 10 April 1963 Harold Macmillan and John F. Kennedy signed the Nassau Agreement, allowing Britain to purchase the A3 missile system.

It should be noted that prior to the 1979 General Election, the Conservative Party stated that if elected they would replace the Polaris missiles with Trident. In 1980, at Washington, the agreement was signed to purchase the Trident C1/C4 missile. In March 1982, the Government decided to buy the upgraded Trident missile 11 D5.

These missiles were to be housed in a British designed and built submarine. Early operating experience with HMS *Valiant* and HMS *Warspite* showed that, while the plant was quiet – a very desirable characteristic in a submarine, whose primary aim was to remain undetected – the reliability would have to be improved. The timescale for the Polaris programme was such that it allowed little or no time for extensive redesigning of the secondary plant. Commander John Warsop (Later Rear Admiral), who died in 1995, was responsible for simplifying and upgrading the reliability of the secondary plant. The operating history of the Polaris Fleet paid a fitting tribute to the Admiral's work, in fact, of all the features removed from the donor SSN plant, only one was put back by subsequent A&A action. HMS *Resolution* and HMS *Repulse* were built by Vickers Shipbuilding at Barrow-in-Furness. HMS *Renown* and HMS *Revenge* were built at Birkenhead by Cammel Laird.

It was imperative that a shore facility be built to support these submarines and their weapon systems. Several sites within the UK were investigated: Falmouth, Milford Haven and the Gareloch. In the end, Faslane was chosen for the following reasons:

Firstly, the Firth of Clyde had ideal water for submarine exercises, with sheltered but deep water access to the open sea. Moreover, it is geographically neither too close nor too remote from a township. It is also readily accessible by sea, road and rail, and an associated Armaments Depot could be built near by.

Development of the base, at Faslane, commenced in March 1962. The depot ship HMS *Adamant* had moved to Faslane in 1958. Before this, she and the 3rd Submarine Squadron had been at Rothesay. The squadron was initially concerned with anti-submarine training and two frigates were attached to the squadron. The HPT boats were used for evaluation, and training surface ships in tracking and attacking fast underwater targets.

HMS *Ben Nevis* (a converted tank landing ship) had been moved to Faslane on 10 August 1960, and was used as an accommodation ship for technicians and key workers involved in the base's construction.

During January 1962, Metal Industries obtained a thirty-year lease on the land at the north end of the base, and at this time were the largest employers on the Gareloch. HMS *Explorer* was decommissioned at Faslane on 5 March 1962.

On 24 May 1962 HMS *Maidstone* relieved HMS *Adamant* as depot ship to the Third Squadron at Faslane. HMS *Maidstone* had been refitted to enable her to support nuclear submarines. The first nuclear powered submarine, HMS *Dreadnought* joined the Squadron in

1963, and had to make second approach to the berth on her arrival. Tragedy stuck the embryonic base on 8 May 1963, when The Vista Club (NAAFI) burnt down. The club was originally opened in 1959.

On 21 May 1963, the Government placed orders for the Polaris submarines, and the major works began at Faslane a day later.

Work started on the Polaris School on 3 January 1964. The school was opened on 30 June 1966, thus avoiding the need to send people to the United States to the USN Guided Missile School at Dam Neck, Virginia. Later in 1964, the Ministry of Works announced in June that the armaments depot for the Polaris submarines would be built at Coulport. On 10 July 1964 building started on the AFD 60 at Portsmouth Dockyard. A year later, on 4 October 1965, the A814 road diversion around the base was opened. On 18 April 1966, the Central Reprographic Services opened for business in the Polaris School. This section can probably lay claim to being the most 'rehoused' unit in the base.

The year 1967 was full and busy for the base. February saw the first Captain of the 10th Submarine Squadron appointed and by the end of March the base was commissioned. On 10 August 1967 the base was officially commissioned, with the formal opening being held on 10 May 1968 by HM Queen Elizabeth. The base was now officially known as the Clyde Submarine Base, HMS *Neptune*. HMS *Resolution* joined the 10th Squadron on 10 June 1967. Captain Kent moved ashore from HMS *Maidstone* and assumed the title Commander, Clyde Submarine Base.

During this period facilities were developed ashore to support the new Polaris submarines that would formed the 10th Submarine Squadron (HMS *Renown*, HMS *Resolution*, HMS *Repulse* and HMS *Revenge*). When the base was commissioned in 1967, the 3rd Submarine Squadron consisted of HMS *Dreadnought*, HMS *Valiant* and HMS *Warspite*. The three improved

HMS *Maidstone* alongside the jetty.

Valiant-class submarines joined shortly after (HMS *Conqueror*, HMS *Churchill* and HMS *Courageous*). The diesel-powered submarine HMS *Oracle* was also part of the 3rd Squadron.

HMS *Maidstone* finally left Faslane on 23 January 1968. Perhaps to make amends, the Services Cinema Corporation opened a temporary cinema at Faslane, just to the south of south gate, on 18 February 1968. AFD 60 undertook its first of over 600 dockings on 10 May 1968, while HMS *Otter* was the dock's first customer. 1968 also saw the Polaris patrol. HMS *Resolution* sailed on 15 June 1968 on what was the first of 229 deterrent patrols, and on the domestic front Provost Williamson opened the new Churchill Estate Community Centre, Supermarket and Drumfolk Club on 13 August 1968. On 22 May 1969, 730 houses were handed over to the MOD at the Churchill Estate. The Sportsdome was opened by Bobby McGregor on 18 March 1969, followed by the Dry Ski Slope, which was completed on 26 March 1969.

The Base complement in June 1969 was 6,541, divided as follows:

Service	HMS *Neptune*	1,215
	3 SM	1,234
	10 SM	1,654
Civilian	Faslane	964
	Coulport	822
MOD Police	Faslane	78
	Coulport	87
Eng Ser	Faslane	311
	Coulport	176

On 30 June 1969 the RAF formally handed over the responsibility for the nuclear deterrent to the Royal Navy.

The early 1970s were particularly unpleasant years for submariners. On 10 Mar 1970 the Tot was stopped, and when it appeared things could not get worse, CSST was formed on 10 October 1973. The only highlight in these dark years was on 15 July 1971, when SM brooches were first issued. The Civilian Canteen was opened on 10 May 1974.

The First Sea Lord visits the Squadron Club during his visit to the base in May 1966.

ROPE introduces BXO on the steps of Balernock House, May 1966.

The first stages of construction at the southern end of the base during 1964.

HMS *Maidstone*'s bow can just be seen in the left of the picture, taken in June 1966.

The northern end of the base seen in October 1996.

The A814 initially ran along the lochside. This photograph, taken in October 1964, shows some of the work involved in re-routing the road to its present day position.

Work at the northern end of the 'detour', February 1965.

Construction begins for the new A814 bypass in July 1965.

The railway bridge over the A814 taking the railway to Metal Industries in September 1966. It was deemed redundant and was later removed.

The southern base approach road, October 1966.

The southern end of the base, October 1966.

The northern end of the base, June 1966.

This photograph, taken four months after the above, gives some idea of the impressive rate of progress during the base construction.

Faslane Bay, October 1966.

The Mess and Recreation Block under construction.

The Mess and Recreation Block.

The Mess and Recreation Block, looking towards the Gareloch.

The Administration Building under construction.

The Administration Building from Maidstone Road.

The Administration Building. The QMS Lobby was situated here and this was initially the base main gate.

The start of the building of the original sick bay, now the Education and Dental Departments.

The Sick Bay nearing completion. The building on the left is the canteen. In February 1943, Miss Chrystall joined the NAAFI at Invergordon and she was still serving at Faslane in 1968.

This building, which was never completed, was going to be the 'POs Club'. It would be imprudent to comment on the proposed location; next to the Sick Bay and in front of where the base church now stands!

NTD under construction during September 1966.

Naval Stores buildings.

The Polaris School can be seen in the distance.

The Link Building under construction.

Naval Stores buildings.

General view of the site.

The Wardroom under construction.

The Wardroom under construction.

Another view of the Wardroom under construction.

The Wardroom nearing completion.

A busy waterfront scene from August 1976.

The Mess and Recreation block under construction.

NTD nearing completion.

A general site view.

The Police Section House.

The Boiler House.

The EWSD Building.

The approach to the Churchill married quarters estate.

Preparing the site at the Churchill Estate.

The married quarters under construction.

The Naval married quarters at the Churchill Estate.

The officers' married quarters at Smugglers Way.

The quarters at Smugglers' Way under construction.

Following pages: The Canteen is in the background. The picture was taken in September 1965 and shows the tunnel under Maidstone Road being fabricated.

A general site view.

The jetty area.

Building work at the north end of the base.

A busy construction scene at the entrance to the base.

The base at the
height of the
building work.

The base in the
mid-1960s.

HMS *Maidstone* leaves Faslane, January 1968.

HMS *Maidstone* being escorted down the Gareloch.

The accommodation ship HMS *Narvick* leaving Faslane on 22 March 1968.

HMS *Narvick* being escorted down the Gareloch.

Polaris School, 18 February 1965. From left to right: Vice Admiral MacKenzie, Capt. Northley (Chief of Staff, Polaris Executive), Lt Baynes (Resident Officer, Polaris Executive).

HMS *Neptune* Main Gate, 1968. Returning submarine crews had to pass through the tunnel on route to their accommodation blocks. Their arrival was eagerly awaited by members of the Regulating Branch, who would lie in wait at the Main Gate. The practice fell into disrepute after one long-haired, badly dressed, scruffy 'submariner' from HMS *Dreadnought* turned out to be a 'lagger' from Vickers.

April 1968: the accommodation blocks are ready for occupation.

The Polaris School is in the centre of the picture. The Wardroom, HMS *Neptune*, is on the right.

The WRNs' Quarters in 1968.

The Administration Building. NTD can be seen in the distance

The ecumenical church under construction. The Sick Bay can be seen in the background.

The Sick Bay waiting room as it was in 1968.

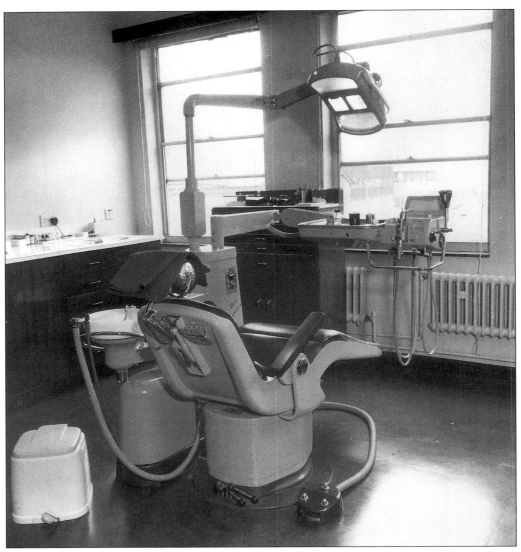

The Dental Department at Faslane – inviting as ever!

What it was all about – the Polaris Missile that graced the entrance to the Polaris School.

The Pay Office, HMS *Neptune*.

Winter 1968, looking towards the mess and recreation block.

Six
1980-1996

On 2 June 1981 the MOD published its proposals for the Trident works development at Faslane and Coulport. On 12 September the Faslane Fair was held in Churchill Square. Later in the year, on 10 October, the MOD repossessed the land leased by Metal Industries. The early 1980s also witnessed the end of American Polaris program. On 2 June 1982 the last missiles were off loaded from USS *Robert E. Lee*.

During May 1984 the MOD submitted plans to the local council for approval of the base development. Gaining approval proved rather difficult and the plans were finally submitted to the Secretary of State for Scotland, Mr George Younger. On 7 March 1985, approval for the MOD plans to develop Faslane to support the Vanguard Class submarines was finally granted.

During the Falklands War, heralded by the illegal Argentinian landing on South Georgia on 19 March 1982, the base was heavily involved in preparing the 3rd Squadron submarines before they deployed to the South Atlantic.

On 10 September 1985, development of the Northern Area at Faslane and the Trident Facilities RNAD Coulport commenced. On 10 July 1987 a major works contract for the construction of the Shiplift, Finger Jetty, Northern Utilities Building (NUB) and associated infrastructure was awarded. Work began on the Shiplift on 24 August 1987, and it was handed over to the MOD on 12 July 1993. On 10 January 1988, the Trident Project Contract was awarded, the main contractor being Norwest Holst Scotland Ltd.

To ease road congestion in the lochside villages during the redevelopment work, two by-pass roads were built. The 17 January 1988 saw the opening of the Garelochhead bypass, shortly followed by the Glen Fruin Haul Road, which was officially opened on 20 January 1988. The year 1988 also signalled the start of the Module Repair and Calibration Facility (MRCF) project, which commenced in September of that year, and is now known as Northern Calibration Facility (NCF). It was completed on 10 February 1990. The General Purpose Support Store (GPSS) was completed on 10 September 1988, and in what was turning out to be a busy year for the base, the first Faslane Fair was held at Helensburgh pier car park on 25 June. A year later, on 15 Feb 1989, Phase One of the Trident Training Facility was completed. The completed facility was opened on 10 July 1990 by the then First Sea Lord, Admiral Sir Julian Oswald.

During May 1990 the refurbishment and upgrading of berths 1 to 6 was started. On 21 May the modernization of 1-4 berths commenced and by 10 Oct that year the 5-6 berth modernization program was completed, and the infilling of the lagoons behind the berths was finished.

On 21 May 1991 the Strategic Weapons Support Building (SWSB) was completed. It was followed, a few weeks later, by the General Services Building (GSB) which was handed over to the MOD on 21 July 1991. This building houses the Vanguard-class submarine's off crews and the Submarine Training Department.

During 1992 the new Medical Centre was opened (10 July) and the Finger Jetty was completed (4 September). The year also saw the Northern Utilities Building (NUB) completed

The new Medical Centre.

(7 October) and by 20 October 1992, the dredging work in Rhu narrows, which was required because of the increased size of the Vanguard-class submarines, was completed.

The MOD Police moved into their new headquarters on 22 March 1994. In 1967 the police operated from Cliffburn Cottage (now the site of the new Srs Mess). By 1970 the CID were working from temporary accommodation opposite the EWSD building. The police dogs (or initially a black Labrador named 'Bohea') lived at the back of the middle gate.

On 10 June 1993 AFD 60 docked its 600th customer and July saw the NTD works nearing completion. The Northern Development Area Trident Support Facilities were officially opened by Malcolm Rifkind, Secretary of State for Defense, on 19 August 1993.

On 1 October 1993 the 3rd and 10th Submarine Squadrons combined to emerge as the First Submarine Squadron (SM1). The new Captain SM1 was Captain McLees who was formally Captain SM3.

The base's complement on 1 July 1996 was:

Service ashore/afloat	4,000	
Civilian staff, Faslane		2,100
Civilian staff, Coulport		1,900
Contractors	3,000	

On 1 October 1996 the Clyde Submarine Base became HM Naval Base Clyde, and so the story of a submarine base is told. But what does the future hold? The elevation of the base to 2* status with the Flag Officer Scotland, Northern England and Northern Ireland transferring his Flag from Pitreavie to Faslane, the integration of HM Naval Base Clyde and the Business Area of the Director Supply North and the arrival of the minor warships, coupled to the numerous other changes the base has witnessed during the last few years, herald what will undoubtedly be a busy and interesting time for all concerned.

The Clyde Submarine Base in the early 1980s.

The Southern end of the base.

The start of the Northern area development in the early 1990s.

Constructing the Finger Jetty.

First stages of the construction of the Shiplift.

The Shiplift nearing completion.

The Shiplift and Finger Jetty.

The interior view of the Shiplift.

The Shiplift nearing completion.

The Clyde Submarine Base from the south.

Seven

The 3rd Submarine Squadron

The Squadron was first formed in 1912 and was known as the 3rd Submarine Flotilla. The squadron was based at Immingham. The term flotilla was dropped after the Second World War in keeping with the tradition adopted by the other NATO countries.

At the start of the Second World War, the Depot Ship HMS *Forth* with the Second Submarine Squadron (eight S-class, three T-class, *Thames*, *Oberon* and *Oxley*) and went to Dundee. The old depot ship HMS *Titania* was sent to Blyth (where she was stationed in the closing stages of the First World War). She had with her the 6th Flotilla (three U-class, three L-class and one H). In all, they were just twenty-one operational submarines in home waters, and five of them were over ten years old. The 5th Submarine Flotilla (eight H-class) remained in Portsmouth for training.

It was decided to create another squadron in home waters to be known as the 3rd Flotilla, by bringing home four S-class submarines from Malta and basing them at Harwich with the old depot ship HMS *Cyclops*.

The fall of France and the invasion of Norway called for a repositioning of the various squadrons. A small operational squadron was formed at Portsmouth to carry out patrols in the Channel. A much larger flotilla was based on the Clyde on the depot ship HMS *Forth*, which had arrived from Rosyth. The flotilla's operational area included the Bay of Biscay. The Harwich Flotilla went to the Clydeand the S-class vessels joined the Flotilla based on HMS *Forth*, while the older H-class were employed in training during anti-submarine escorts.

After the Second World War the Squadron was based at Rothesay, where it was responsible for training and the development of tactics. On 9 September 1957, HMS *Adamant* and the 3rd Squadron left Rothesay to take part in NATO exercises and on their return in mid-October the squadron transferred to Faslane.

On 19 March 1982, the Argentinians illegally landed on South Georgia, the precursor to what became the Falklands conflict. The Fleet submarines of the 3rd Squadron played an important role in the conflict. HMS *Conqueror* sank the Argentinian cruiser *Belgrano* on 2 May 1982. HMS *Warspite* spent 114 days away from the base; HMS *Courageous* was the first Sub-Harpoon-equipped vessel in the area.

Depot Ships of the 3rd Submarine Squadron

30 Jun 1940	HMS *Forth*
25 May 1947	HMS *Montclare*
20 Sep 1954	HMS *Adamant*
24 May 1962	HMS *Maidment*
6 Jan 1969	HMS *Neptune*

The crest of the 3rd Submarine Squadron.

Submarines loading torpedoes at Immingham, 1913.

HMS *Cyclops*, an ex-Indrabarah, was in the Mediterranean until 1939 when she was called home to become the Depot Ship to the 3rd Flotilla. She was launched on 27 October 1905 and finally scrapped at Newport in July 1947.

HMS *Forth* in the Holy Loch during the Second World War.

HMS *Montclare* and her sister ship HMS *Montcalm* (ex-Wolfe) were two AMCs purchased from the Canadian Pacific Steamship Co. and converted to submarine depot ships. This is HMS *Montclare* in Rothesay Bay, May 1948.

HMS *Montclare* at Rothesay.

HMS *Adamant*, 1956.

HMS *Maidstone* as she was during the war.

HMS *Forth*. She was launched at the John Brown shipyard, Clydebank, on 11 August 1938. In September 1939 she was home to the 2nd Flotilla at Dundee and, due to the lack of air defence, was ordered to Rosyth with the 2nd and 6th flotillas. She was briefly in the Clyde in 1941 before going to Halifax. By January 1942, HMS *Forth* was back in the Clyde.

HMS *Conqueror*, returning from the Falklands in July 1982 after the attack on the *Belgrano*. The submarine had to take evasive action to avoid the counterattack. Once everything had returned to normal, the 1st Lieutenant walked around the boat. On arriving at the Senior Rates Mess, he enquired if 'anything had moved?' 'Only bowels, Sir' was the reply!

HMS *Churchill*.

HMS *Valiant*, the first totally
'homegrown' nuclear
submarine.

HMS *Odin*, one of the 3rd Submarine Squadron's conventionally powered submarines.

Eight

The 10th Submarine Squadron

The 10th Submarine Flotilla was formed during December 1914 at Devonport and based on the depot ship HMS *Forth*. The flotilla remained at Devonport until it was disbanded on 2 March 1919. The depot ships associated with the flotilla during this period were:

10 December 1914	HMS *Forth*
3 July 1916	HMS *Vulcan*
20 August 1916	HMS *Lucia*

During the Second World War, the flotilla was re-formed at Malta on 1 September 1941. The base was HMS *Talbot* at Manoul Island in Grand Harbor. Before being disbanded on 21 September 1944, the 'Fighting 10th' had sunk or damaged 1,056,000 tons of enemy shipping. The flotilla's small U-class submarines severely disrupted the enemy supply lines to Northern Africa and played a major role in the successful outcome of the North African campaign.

During the siege of Malta, the submarines had to dive alongside the quay during the day to avoid the heavy German bombing. They would surface in the evening to charge their batteries and continue with the maintenance and repair work. During 1941 and 1942, nineteen of the Squadron's submarines were lost on operations in the Mediterranean. A further four were sunk alongside during the heavy bombing in March and April 1942. It may be sobering to reflect that in these times Submarine Pay was three shillings a day!

The submarines and their crews passed into submarine 'folklore'; Perhaps the most famous of them was Lt Cdr Wanklyn VC DSO of HMS *Upholder*, lost after twenty-five gruelling patrols, but with a remarkable 135,000 tons of enemy shipping to his credit. Also Lt Cdr Mars DSO DSC of HMS *Unbroken*, who destroyed a train in a gun action!

All through September 1944, submarines of the 10th Flotilla were committed to other flotillas. A majority went to the 1st Flotilla in the eastern Mediterranean, while the remained were sent to the Eastern Fleet Flotilla in Ceylon.

The Squadron was re-formed at Faslane on 1 February 1967, and eventually consisted of four Polaris submarines. Between 15 June 1968 and 13 May 1996, the submarines of the 10th Squadron carried out a total of 229 Polaris patrols, which involved the submarines steaming in excess of two million miles. A submarine of the 10th Squadron (HMS *Resolution*) holds the somewhat dubious honor of having completed the longest period submerged for any operational submarine. On two consecutive patrols the submarine remained submerged for more than 2,400 hours. To put that figure in some sort of perspective, most fish don't spend that long under the sea!

During the 1990s the Polaris submarines were gradually replaced by the newer Vanguard-class Trident submarines. On 26 May 1994, HMS *Vanguard* fired the first two British Trident missiles off Florida. Later in the year, on 19 July, HMS *Resolution* was decommissioned. On 13 May 1996 HMS *Repulse* completed the last Polaris deterrent patrol. Her official decommissioning was held in the Northern Development Area and the ceremony combined with the 'End of Polaris' service.

The crest of the 10th Submarine Squadron when it was re-formed as the Polaris Squadron.

HMS *Forth*, the 10th flotilla's depot ship from 10 December 1914 to 2 July 1916.

HMS *Vulcan*, depot ship from 3 July 1916 to 19 August 1916.

HMS *Lucia*, depot ship from 20 August 1916 to 2 March 1919.

The 10th Submarine's Flotilla's wartime base in Malta, HMS *Talbot* on Manoul Island in Valletta harbour.

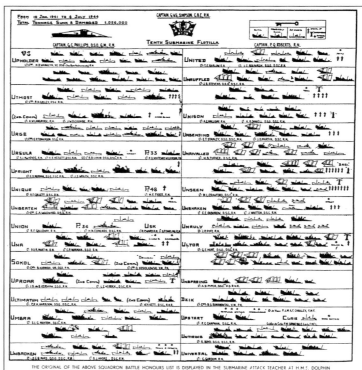

The 10th Submarine Flotilla's record of tonnage sunk and damaged from 10 January 1941 to 4 July 1944, while the Flotilla was stationed at Malta.

Submarines of the 10th Flotilla at Malta during 1941. HMS *Ursula* is on the left of the picture, while Lt Cdr Wanklyn's HMS *Upholder* is on the right.

Malta, 1942. Submarines of the 10th Flotilla alongside their base at Manuol Island, Malta.

A Polaris missile launched by HMS *Renown* (Starboard) crew, 24 July 1964.

The *Hi Ho Journal*, HMS *Renown* (Starboard) ship company's weekly magazine, produced during her first commission. Most submarines produce a 'mag', and all of them operate by the good journalistic practice of 'not letting the truth get in the way of a good story.'

HMS *Repulse* coming alongside
at Faslane after her maiden
voyage to Barrow.

A Polaris submarine undergoing
maintenance in the base's
Floating Dock.

An unusual view of the Polaris fleet, or at least, three-quarters of the Polaris fleet!

HMS *Resolution* leaving Faslane in October 1992.

A gull's eye view of HMS *Repulse*.

The launch of a
Trident missile.